Writing Prompts for Creative Writers

By Levon Sparks Salone

Kindle Edition 2014

Copyright ©2014 Levon Sparks Salone

Other Books by Levon Sparks Salone

Fiction:

Waltzing With Deception (The Chillings Series, Book 1)

Unjust Ruling (The Chillings Series, Book 2)

Non-Fiction:

Men Hurt Too!

Writing Prompts for Creative Writers

Book Contents:

50 Writing Prompts
25 Key Words for Each Prompt

How to Use This Book:

Writers can create stories of varying lengths:

500 Words
750 Words
1000 Words
Unlimited (Per Writer's or Instructor's Discretion)

Writers can use all or some of the Key Words in each story.

10 Words
15 Words
25 Words

Writers should use each Key Word as listed. (Do not substitute **laughing** for **laugh** or **sandwiches** for **sandwich**.)

Examples of Instructions:

Write a 750-word story from Prompt 15. Use all 25 Key Words.
Write a 1000-word story from Prompt 20. Use 15 Key Words.
Write a 2500-word story from Prompt 29. Use all 25 Key Words.

(When you have completed your story, give it a title.)

NOTE: This workbook is not a teaching tool. Its purpose is to assist in the creative writing process.

Prompts

Prompt 1

Jennifer Ann Nottingham didn't believe in aliens ... until today.

Key Words

Trap	Bat	Booth	Medieval	Equal
Sorry	Equal	Human	Bolt	Heroic
Rammed	Basket	Baton	Basement	Billfold
Immense	Garden	Bomb	Butter	Bifocals
List	Bilingual	Briar	Marble	Buoyant

Your Story

Prompt 2

Katie was a beautiful woman before the accident.

Key Words

Cherish	Circled	Intake	Unbeliever	Manipulator
O'clock	Installment	Integrity	Driveway	Entrusted
Insomnia	Religious	Faith	Slave	Whisper
Professor	Request	Quiz	Boring	Racket
Fool	Feelings	Poverty	Midst	Hygiene

Your Story

Prompt 3

The cool breeze blew through her window, but something about its flow signaled danger.

Key Words

Blister	Institute	Precede	Flashback	Below
Prosperous	Respectful	Resist	Roar	Traitor
Trample	Flare	Inspire	Branch	Near
Instant	Fainted	Pound	Howl	Case
Sneaky	Shine	Shell	Resign	Ask

Your Story

Prompt 4

Kevin Jones left town with his bags on his back, promising never to return to his cursed roots.

Key Words

Miserly	Weightless	Vapor	Simple	Tabletop
Dodge	Trace	Infamous	Finite	Pauper
Extreme	Tray	Wince	Seven	Weep
Struggle	Laughter	Slick	Turmoil	Peppy
Slander	Noble	Trick	Slide	Torment

Your Story

Prompt 5

He scanned the audience, hoping she wouldn't be there, but Margie Timms sat on the back row, waiting to make her move.

Key Words

Guardian	Isolate	Extended	Socialization	Pout
Temperature	Upbeat	Bother	Urban	Engaging
Irresistible	Flatter	Skill	Graciously	Audacious
Timid	Stony	Height	Drenched	Upstairs
Elegant	Meek	Sticky	Vehicle	Moist

Your Story

Prompt 6

Alexander Charles Townsend, an elitist, used to sneer at the homeless; he never thought he would be one of them.

Key Words

Holiday	Virus	Chaos	Handout	Weapon
Household	Twisted	Apparatus	Strawberries	Punches
Zealous	Weather	Storm	Box	Detective
Amputate	Angle	Filthy	Cracked	Resume
Ceiling	Shelter	Automobile	Ancient	Shouldn't

Your Story

Prompt 7

It was a family secret, and Sylvia pledged to take it with her to the grave.

Key Words

Emotions	Introduced	Paranoid	Escape	Extra
Weak	Powerful	Dumped	Convenient	Swirled
Veto	Final	Vibrant	Web	Circumstances
Magnify	Mahogany	Humor	Minutes	Firearm
View	Aligned	Magazine	Regretted	Irate

Your Story

Prompt 8

Hazel Dana Simpson took a chance and lost it all.

Key Words

Breakfast	Daisy	Youngsters	Urban	Cracked
Complimentary	Footprints	Printed	Continuous	Music
Gigantic	Omelets	Allegiance	Pathway	Payment
Loan	Reader	Function	Tournament	Horizon
Taste	Steam	Debt	Practice	Messy

Your Story

Prompt 9

She never dated across political lines, but something about Charles Abbot made her take the risk.

Key Words

Will	Wrinkle	Dumbest	Narrow	Worldly
Academics	Compensation	Zest	Window	Opportunity
Expelled	School	Manners	Death	Makeover
Companions	Opposition	Assistant	Heaviness	Tiresome
Technical	Trio	Volcano	Tinkle	Unconscious

Your Story

Prompt 10

Everything Henry Collins touched turned to gold, even the people he loved.

Key Words

Rope	Skeleton	Kindest	Threat	Usage
Produced	Common	Topaz	Snob	Superstition
Theory	Stole	Blocked	Skipped	Hurdle
Vanished	Quantities	Tropical	Ladder	Tender
Savor	Contradict	Possessive	Gamble	Solitary

Your Story

Prompt 11

Jessica's parents were strict, and if she followed their rules, she would never date the hottest guy on the football team.

Key Words

Serious	Temper	Biased	Worry	Dismissal
Traveler	Special	Party	Paddle	Shady
Sweating	Pester	Pointed	Thirsty	Money
Sharp	Pastel	Flatter	Delight	Nudge
Drool	Muscular	School	Strong	Snapped

Your Story

Prompt 12

He never knew being rich would cause so much pain.

Key Words

Adults	Parachute	Underfoot	Shack	Public
Dying	Similar	Flashy	Duchess	Soda
Offering	Bridge	Blade	Chiefly	Sinister
Duration	Fiesta	Congregate	Tramps	Style
Halo	Hunter	Goblet	Factory	Constrict

Your Story

Prompt 13

Catherine's day started with a bang.

Key Words

Nature	Moist	Swollen	Tempter	Search
Tracked	Biceps	Promise	Swift	Productive
Neat	Secret	Swivel	Solid	Week
Thankful	Calculator	Charity	Charisma	Wet
Ton	Project	Best	Earrings	Below

Your Story

Prompt 14

Patrick Woods had a huge following on the internet, but if his followers only knew…

Key Words

Pictures	Choices	Unlimited	Sheepishly	Movie
Average	Stunning	Expensive	Negatively	Swipe
Networks	Retrieved	Blog	Pressure	Journal
Feast	Urgent	World	Tossed	Ceremony
Holidays	Avoidance	Freedom	Activate	Tempo

Your Story

Prompt 15

Lindsey prayed for a miracle and received more than she expected.

Key Words

Opinions	Impeccably	Gridlock	Shoulder	Confident
Persistent	Destined	Stranger	Extraordinary	Private
Busybody	Burner	Owner	Elbowed	Resort
Siblings	Balloons	Wholesale	Castaway	Canteen
Idiot	Glare	Commitment	Cardboard	Century

Your Story

Prompt 16

The maid prepared a magnificent dinner, but two hours after eating it, Sterling couldn't move his legs.

Key Words

Clockwork	Small	Enclosure	Telephone	Audience
Nail	Laser	Pollute	Stomach	Large
Clothes	Lapse	Energy	Comply	Slow
Pony	Tickle	Ears	Fast	Audio
Clog	Portrayal	Intelligence	Futuristic	Questionable

Your Story

Prompt 17

No one believed Abbie's story, except the blind five-year-old girl.

Key Words

Leftovers	Sexist	Racist	Quote	Operation
Legacy	Wealth	Labor	Lacquer	Lemonade
Contemptible	Quit	Ceiling	Straws	Bitterness
Family	Language	Sneezed	Lenient	Prudent
Motive	Kingdom	Smashed	Memorial	Member

Your Story

Prompt 18

Loretta vowed to quit her bad habit; her life depended on it.

Key Words

Pure	Battle	Careful	Obituary	Random
Accident	Scary	Destination	Permission	Reassurance
Moaned	Pious	Lyrics	Persuade	Syndrome
Invisible	Suicide	Mistakes	Wager	Lecture
Decode	Terror	Grudge	Growth	Vulnerability

Your Story

Prompt 19

She told Robin that Bob abandoned them. Was that the truth, or did her mother lie about that too?

Key Words

Unreasonable	Image	Forbidden	Excuses	Coordinate
Bicker	Awe	Appreciate	Approach	Cord
Sick	Leaned	Glitch	Motionless	Version
Mirror	Darkness	Disguise	Decorator	Coroner
Phony	Nodded	Masculine	Pitiful	Ruthless

Your Story

Prompt 20

Joanna feared facing the judge; she knew her fate rested in his hands.

Key Words

Testimony	Immediate	Promiscuity	Augment	Autobiography
Breathtaking	Papers	Attractive	Daylight	Life
Entrance	Daughters	Average	Ballot	Banish
Burnt	Middle	Obscene	Childlike	Autumn
Sons	Justified	Afflict	Catastrophe	Bible

Your Story

Prompt 21

"Stop!" Roger yelled. "You can't go in there!"

Key Words

Road	Heads	Airplane	Rug	Aroma
Pistol	Fingers	Split	Joined	Collar
Bookish	Checkbook	Clot	Badge	Mount
Gloves	Constitution	Disaster	Fixture	Frugal
Incubate	Minor	Blue	Cried	Marquee

Your Story

Prompt 22

Millicent enjoyed attending Mount Moriah until she heard Pastor Hill's third sermon.

Key Words

Servant	Integrity	Commandments	Hypocrite	Judge
Slander	Sinful	Conceited	Reputation	Criticism
Discover	Evil	Neighbor	Tongue	Unruly
Love	Spiritual	Torch	Lawlessness	Holy
Personal	Wrong	Forgiveness	Repent	Congregants

Your Story

Prompt 23

Randy wrote the perfect love song for Miranda, but he was too ashamed to give it to her.

Key Words

Guidance	Flexible	Brainstorm	Scarf	Sober
Celebrate	Paraphrase	Dialogue	Blueprint	Border
Circular	Mobile	Status	Grandmother	Invited
Together	Fire	Variety	Diction	Multitasking
Elementary	Ruined	Salty	Unique	Scarce

Your Story

Prompt 24

Cynthia finally got pregnant, but instead of showing support, Frank became jealous.

Key Words

Contempt	Coherent	Regulations	Abound	Chivalry
Witnesses	Bachelor	Argue	Deafening	Cripple
Outsiders	Promised	Different	Covenant	Contagious
Crisis	Wreck	Transformed	Counteract	Tremble
Veiled	Vaulted	Zombie	Optimize	Alien

Your Story

Prompt 25

"Revenge, revenge, revenge," she whispered before placing her head under the blanket and falling asleep.

Key Words

Splendor	Addiction	Physician	Shy	Hallway
Alarm	Shrewd	Hospital	Crowd	Sedan
Nurse	Medicine	Needle	Showroom	Surface
Slice	Revoke	Riddle	Watch	Rifle
Seesaw	Western	Pills	Militant	Outwardly

Your Story

Prompt 26

"Could Addie Mae Nettles date a poor man?"

Key Words

Strenuous	Sporty	Exposed	Gentle	Pretended
Tractor	Sheep	Snooze	Browsed	Laughter
Standard	Sunlight	Outlet	Stallion	Beast
Barn	Bruised	Reflective	Blazed	Knot
Prompt	Attire	Submerge	Subtle	Stampede

Your Story

Prompt 27

The fight lasted fifteen minutes, but it seemed like hours.

Key Words

Flawless	Atmosphere	Summary	Sudden	Tickets
Urgent	Untangle	Vulgar	Frustrated	Paper
Sported	Throne	Plugged	Volunteer	Necessary
Shouted	Rigid	Loyal	Thriller	Overrun
Swayed	Belongings	Reign	Slogan	Pump

Your Story

Prompt 28

Two women dating one man is a recipe for disaster.

Key Words

Eleven	Dinner	Deadline	Grave	Burial
Elastic	Belly	Stretches	December	Desert
Deprive	Elegant	Fangs	Broached	Southern
Sidetracked	Painful	Porch	Inhaled	Secondary
Suffer	Solely	Latest	Latin	Hobnob

Your Story

Prompt 29

Lucinda told Mark that secret in confidence. She didn't think he would post it in *The Mulberry's Gazette*.

Key Words

Divorce	Mentioned	Favorite	Waitress	Personal
Allocate	Friendly	Antisocial	Proved	Dreams
Dispense	Problem	Scatter	Apartment	Beginning
Supersede	Backfire	Barrier	Appeased	Applaud
Traveled	Haste	Stall	Backward	Barren

Your Story

Prompt 30

"Benjamin cried wolf for the last time!" Sharon yelled at the mirror as she thought about her wayward son.

Key Words

Betrayal	References	Fake	Outlaw	Worthless
Prototype	Legalize	Approachable	Address	Thumb
Individual	Trust	Eject	Frequently	Popular
Aloof	Usually	Adolescent	Expelled	Secure
Speech	Alert	Horoscope	Lovesick	Optional

Your Story

Prompt 31

Ida Pecker married the richest man in the county, but her heart was with Rufus, the farmer who lived across town.

Key Words

Unauthorized	Bumper	Better	Mountains	Purple
Dilemma	Foul	Volume	Amateur	Broken
Translation	Against	Fried	Protected	Jewel
Business	Arrested	Purchased	Religious	Pattern
Title	Fortune	Calculating	Primary	Sunflowers

Your Story

Prompt 32

Johnny never thought he would see the day when he had to choose between his dog and his girlfriend.

Key Words

Somersault	Slash	Awkward	Prospect	Drastic
Incompetent	Stern	Sober	Property	Cruel
Educated	Eccentric	Trembling	Traitor	Sprout
Refined	Garage	Staircase	Tossed	Pointless
Infrastructure	Immediate	Deescalate	Fabric	Cheeks

Your Story

Prompt 33

Simeon tried not to laugh, but a giggle escaped his lips.

Key Words

Miracle	Savage	Never	Many	Sales
Reason	Trainer	Knees	Sulk	Uneven
Pencils	Clerk	Transportation	Comedy	Sullen
Flavors	Flapped	Interior	Lighting	Massive
Ogle	Prediction	Clapped	Teased	Towels

Your Story

Prompt 34

Doreen loved the red dress; it reminded her of the past.

Key Words

Pinned	Dense	Coward	Actress	Abhor
Flirt	Coherent	Touchy	Pimple	Drained
Taboo	Slippers	Disposal	Genie	Generalize
Kinetic	Ivy	Passionate	Striking	Strategy
Helm	Fabulous	Designed	Expressions	Lingered

Your Story

Prompt 35

Todd told the lie so many times; he started to believe it.

Key Words

Car	Wagon	Yellow	Violent	Intern
Jokingly	Omen	Maintained	Peace	Children
Jerk	Strangle	Streak	Suppress	Lizard
Logical	Locate	Kookaburra	Emerald	Grindstone
Grenade	Orange	Necktie	Proverb	Proofread

Your Story

Prompt 36

Ashlyn had to make her marriage work if she wanted to land the position of partner at her firm.

Key Words

Lonely	Feast	Gallivanting	Gladness	Faithful
Thief	Deliver	Abhorrent	Vessels	Instructions
Extended	Rib	Rebuke	Wiser	Evening
Collapsed	Rainbow	Lying	Honored	Generation
Thousand	Provider	Scarlet	Scandal	Stale

Your Story

Prompt 37

Eleanor witnessed a miracle, one that stripped away her hatred.

Key Words

Unspeakable	Flushed	Desserts	Strings	Temple
Flooded	Landscape	Women	Dusty	Seasoning
Peppers	Purpose	Inhabitants	Counseled	Armies
Shields	Boots	War	Scarred	Warrior
Lighter	Ruler	Highway	Gleaming	Noon

Your Story

Prompt 38

"Life is full of surprises. Wait until you hear about mine."

Key Words

Hesitate	Fireplace	Happy	Praise	Fireworks
Chocolate	Keen	Escalated	Heyday	Faint
Fantastic	Intensity	Robbed	Victory	Truce
Firsthand	Kerchief	Sitcom	Percentage	Vocalist
Virtue	Single	Silverware	Psychological	Trophy

Your Story

Prompt 39

Meredith loved the movie, but if she had it her way, she would change the ending.

Key Words

Canary	Luxury	Battle	Central	Twist
Anchor	Ancestors	Computers	Distribute	Garments
Blind	Lyrics	Gardens	Nomads	Jogging
Blurb	Sixteen	Overflow	Climax	Arena
Banished	Verses	Finished	Expert	Inaccessible

Your Story

Prompt 40

Jim had no idea what awaited him after retirement.

Key Words

Balm	Regardless	Stagger	Mighty	Merry
Consecrate	Reach	Metamorphosis	Melody	Intuition
Merciful	Serious	Crabby	Merged	Chamber
Photo	Touched	Factory	Subordinate	Appraisal
Loathed	Order	Requests	Lessons	Genuine

Your Story

Prompt 41

The lion clawed at the tree, grasping to rip the flesh from the hunter's leg.

Key Words

Mighty	Dangerous	Strict	Mouthwatering	Expired
Whooping	Primitive	Wrestle	Manmade	Windy
Thicket	Marred	Masterful	Widespread	Wooded
Adventurous	Texture	Metabolism	Rain	Benevolent
Berries	Concoct	Earthly	Stalked	Morbid

Your Story

Prompt 42

Marcus maxed out his credit cards to impress Debra. So why was she dating Billy Jackson?

Key Words

Banjo	Cancelled	Camouflaged	Coherent	Coffee
Cushioned	Sensitivity	Bench	Bandanna	Reports
Cultured	Logbook	Chronicles	Courtyard	Idols
Persona	Perturb	Refinished	Voucher	Wedding
Cuddly	Egocentric	Dormitory	Coronary	Budget

Your Story

Prompt 43

"I know seasons change, but this summer seemed to last longer than usual."

Key Words

Drape	Plant	Radiant	Tense	Parasite
Partner	Meadow	Tight-fisted	Participate	Parents
Wine	Prowl	Slippery	Greedy	Responsible
Tourist	Sandwiches	Bubbling	Chanting	Unlocked
Imagined	Philosophy	Headquarters	Pitiful	Ravenous

Your Story

Prompt 44

They told her she was a witch, and she believed them.

Key Words

Stigma	Serpent	Kissed	Blueprints	Patron
Magical	Suspenseful	Misadventures	Centerpiece	Bells
Permanently	Plastic	Talented	Signature	Psychic
Visions	Brooch	Wizards	Forgery	Warning
Brain	Innocence	Exasperation	Unsurpassed	Walls

Your Story

Prompt 45

Kelvin turned the ignition for the third time, but his '67 Chevy refused to crank.

Key Words

Pedestrian	Horn	Rusty	Liar	Uniforms
Thuggish	Avert	Barked	Informer	Womanly
Weekend	Enthusiast	Madman	Directions	Smoke
Surface	Thrashing	Discreet	Neighbors	Indifferent
Handsome	Vanities	Homesick	Slipping	Turquoise

Your Story

Prompt 46

Five of them went out; four of them returned.

Key Words

Brilliant	Pipe	Spectacles	Armchair	Mortgage
Negotiate	Pinched	Renovator	Crime	Birds
Weapon	Examined	Twigs	Shovel	Euphoria
Impetuous	Grunted	Slingshot	Channels	Blanket
Fragile	Smugglers	Scampered	Crooks	Dungeons

Your Story

Prompt 47

The horse-drawn carriage pulled in front of the dilapidated barn. Mr. Cox allowed his eyes to scan the ruins.

Key Words

Plain	Locally	Backward	Primitive	Tribal
Province	Downfall	Reins	Corrupted	Squabble
Buttons	Shanty	Complaints	Shoulders	Hooked
Curtains	Adhere	Heaven	Stars	Stove
Letters	Pregnant	Massaged	Objections	Daily

Your Story

Prompt 48

She could keep the money or her soul, but she couldn't have both.

Key Words

Midnight	Country	Bats	Queer	Storms
Enormous	Picturesque	Distress	Elderly	Archway
Supper	Disposal	Nationalities	Peasants	Black
Modesty	English	Brushed	Castle	Pearls
Ship	Mystery	Dimensions	Vintage	Horror

Your Story

Prompt 49

Business was Thelma's middle name, and she had one week to convince Mr. Hillshire she was the woman for the job.

Key Words

Corporate	Products	Upgrades	Professional	Cyberspace
Reports	Information	Comprehensive	Nodded	Prescribed
Bylaws	Appointments	Samples	Premonition	Sect
Buffer	Nickname	Slender	Bullied	Support
Trauma	Injured	Courts	Unearthed	Watchdog

Your Story

Prompt 50

Madam Carter had Sean thrown in jail, but she couldn't incarcerate the truth.

Key Words

Genetics	Terrorism	Cloning	Planet	Conspiracy
Bully	Imprisonment	Rehabilitation	Testimony	Clinical
Functioning	Profile	Apprehension	Agencies	Charts
Groups	Mentality	Assumptions	Deception	Justice
Errors	Beginners	Navigated	Guilty	Released

Your Story

Hope you enjoyed the journey!

Levon

www.ingramcontent.com/pod-product-compliance
Lightning Source LLC
Chambersburg PA
CBHW051946280526

45789CB00009B/3182